BRUEGEL

BRUEGEL

PAINTINGS

Introduction by
Arturo Bovi

Geddes & Grosset

Translated by Christopher Clark
Edited and adapted by Colin Clark

First published 1977
© 1977 Nardini Editore, Centro
Internazionale del Libro SpA, Florence,
Italy
© 1977 Giunti Marzocco SpA, Florence,
Italy
First published in this edition 1990
Published by Geddes & Grosset Ltd,
David Dale House,
New Lanark, Scotland
© Geddes & Grosset Ltd

ISBN 1 85534 001 1

Printed in Yugoslavia

CONTENTS

Bruegel

Like most Netherlandish artists of his time,
Pieter Bruegel travelled to Italy to learn
from the masters of the Italian Renais-
sance. Little is evident in his work of the art
of Italy, but he did return with two important souvenirs — a memory of majestic
landscapes, particularly in the Alps, and a
knowledge of the technique of miniature
painting acquired from the Dalmatian
miniaturist, Giulio Clovio, a technique
that, combined with his own personal
vision and understanding of people, was to
stand him in good stead.

Twelve Netherlandish Proverbs (Antwerp)
is a series of twelve roundels that each
depict a proverb enacted by a figure. The
same theme led to the more ambitious
Netherlandish Proverbs (Berlin), his first
important painting to concentrate on

figures rather than landscape. In it are recorded over a hundred proverbs, many unintelligible to the modern viewer, although we can recognize in the man trying to shear a pig the idea that copying another's example is useless unless it is done with intelligence, while the man bashing his head against a brick wall is still rapidly getting nowhere. Already evident are Bruegel's inventiveness and drollery, which made his works popular with collectors of the time, and also his breadth of composition, and his subtle use of colour.

Painted around the same time as each other are two paintings in which it is the landscape that still predominates. In *View of Naples* (Rome) Bruegel's knowledge of weather and landscape, possibly inspired by his friend, the geographer Abraham Ortelius, are put to good effect and combined with accurately and minutely drawn ships, always a great interest of his. A carefully drawn ship also appears in the second, *Landscape with the fall of Icarus*

(Brussels). Bruegel painted two versions of this subject, which tells of the mythical flight of Daedalus and his son Icarus from Crete, using wings made of wax. Icarus flies too near to the sun, his wings melt, and he falls from the sky, illustrating a popular theme — the danger of going to extremes. 'How everything turns away quite leisurely from the disaster' was the poet W. H. Auden's reaction to this painting. In the wide landscape bathed in glorious light, life goes on: the farmer ploughs his furrow, the shepherd watches his sheep; the only indication of the disaster are poor Icarus's legs emerging from the sea.

Breadth of composition is put to good effect in two works (both in Vienna) that share many stylistic traits, including the extra element of Bruegel's growing interest in ordinary people and their labours and pastimes. *The battle between Carnival and Lent*, again a popular theme and seen from the usual Netherlandish high viewpoint, depicts the events of Mardi Gras, when skinny Lent, armed with a griddle on which lie two penitential herrings, comes to chase off corpulent Prince Carnival whose skewer bears fatted capons. Behind each is a train of people representing their theme, and all around are folk having a last Carnival fling, or performing acts of charity, or just going about their daily lives.

Some ninety games feature in the compendious *Children's games*, where, against a background of bold perspective, hundreds of children earnestly and zestfully play at games still recognizable today. It can be viewed as a children's paradise, with no trace of schoolwork or adults, but, as so often with Bruegel, a deeper interpretation can be drawn from the strange physiognomy of some of the figures, the mask of tragedy on the left, and the dominant civic building.

The battle between the Philistines and the Israelites (Vienna) illustrates Bruegel's development in recounting Biblical stories in the costumes and context of his own time. The landscape is rockily Italian in character, while in the foreground the angle of the spears of the Philistine troops on the right indicates all too clearly their success. On the left, the defeated king of the Israelites, Saul, throws himself on his sword rather than be taken prisoner.

For some reason as yet unexplained, Bruegel appears not to have painted anything for a period of about a year, 1561, and when he did return it was with a work in which the influence of his famous compatriot Hieronymous Bosch can clearly be seen, *The fall of the rebel angels* (Brussels). Here are the strange beings, half-human, half-creature, metamorphizing into demonic form as they tumble from heaven towards hell, chased out by an oddly frail armour-clad St Michael, assisted by good angels dressed in white. Bruegel's inspired use of colour is apparent here, from the pale shining light of heaven to the ominous brown tones of hell below.

Two chained monkeys (Berlin) can also be

read as an allegory of the punishment of sin — in this case, humankind trapped by its own frailties. But there could be another interpretation — that the anxious monkeys represent a people held in servitude. It is not impossible that this was Bruegel's view of the Netherlands of the time under the yoke of the repressive Spanish empire.

The great tower of Babel (Vienna) is one of two versions that Bruegel painted of this blasphemous attempt of mankind, described in Genesis, to 'build a city and a tower whose top may reach unto heaven'. God's punishment was to 'confound their language', to remove from them the ability to understand each other. The subject provides the ideal opportunity for an artist concerned with man's weakness and presumption to show that pride can result in exaggeration and folly. The king, on an inspection tour in the foreground, is swamped by the enormity of the over-dominating tower of foolishness.

Although Bruegel moved to Brussels in

1563, he painted *The great tower of Babel* for the Antwerp banker, Niclaes Jonghelinck, a long-time patron, for whom he also painted *The procession to Calvary* (Vienna). Originally titled *Christ carrying the Cross*, it was retitled because of its unusual composition. The tiny figure of Christ struggling under the Cross lies in the centre of the curving composition that suggests the movement of the crowd towards Calvary. In the foreground the two Marys of the New Testament and St John comfort the Virgin Mary, all dressed in the ideal clothes of the subject, in contrast to the crowds around, who are dressed in the normal wear of the time. In the Netherlandish landscape stands an almost Alpine pinnacle of rock surmounted by a windmill, a device long employed by Netherlandish painters as representative of the Cross.

Landscape is forgotten by Bruegel in *The Adoration of the Kings* (London), the painting in which any Italian influence on him is most apparent. It is possible that it was painted for an altarpiece as it is unusual in Bruegel's works in having the proportions of a portrait rather than a landscape. Despite the Italian influence, the work is personal to Bruegel, in its figures which serve almost an architectural function, in its faces, and in the true Bruegel touch of the man whispering in Joseph's ear.

Again for Jonghelinck, Bruegel illustrated the months of the year, in that tradition popular in medieval Europe of depicting man in his relationship with the months and seasons. It is not known how many paintings were originally intended for the series, but five still exist. *Hunters in the snow* (Vienna), the masterpiece that demonstrates Bruegel's equal control of composition as of detail, has a marvellous sense of environment and may represent December and January, while the subdued tones and grey clouds of *Gloomy day* (also Vienna) may be the glum days of February and March. In *Haymaking* (Prague), the fresh green and light yellow are early summer, while the glorious reds and oranges of *Harvest* (New York) convey the burgeoning months of August and September, with the noble tree drawing together a composition of great sweep and imagination. Finally comes autumn in the bare trees and the warm browns of landscape and beasts in *The return of the herd* (Vienna).

Less evident but still there is the influence of Bosch in *The triumph of death* (Madrid), another reminder of the serious nature, amounting almost to pessimism, of Bruegel's view of life. The skeleton hordes of Death conquer all — peasant, cardinal, soldier or knight — while in the background lie other means — fire, execution, shipwreck.

The spirit of Bosch is stronger again in *Dulle Griet ('Mad Meg')* (Antwerp), Bruegel's interpretation of the virago of northern tradition who embodies what were considered the worst aspects of women, malevolence and greed. In peasant dress but protected by armour and sword and carrying ordinary objects from the medieval kitchen, Griet marches towards the strange little monsters issuing from the gaping mouth of a huge fish, symbolic in Netherlandish art of the mouth of hell, with the face of a man. Behind she leaves a melée of women attacking other monsters.

Some have seen a political side to *Dulle Griet,* with the virago as the forces of Erasmus, Reformists and reason against the monsters of superstition, and there may also be a political interpretation to *The numbering at Bethlehem* (Brussels). Painted in 1566, the year when a mass revolt by the people against the power of the Spanish empire led to the sacking of churches, it sets the Biblical story of the census for taxation commanded by imperial decree by Caesar Augustus firmly in a northern, snow-covered Bethelehem. Joseph, carrying a saw, is leading the pregnant Mary seated on a donkey towards the crowd surrounding the tax collectors. Nothing has happened, yet despite the normal activities all around, there is an unsettled atmosphere of tension.

Often seen as a pair with it is *The massacre of the Innocents* (Vienna), the story of how Herod, having heard of the child born in Bethlehem who will be king, 'sent forth and slew all the children that were in Bethlehem'. Again, Bethlehem is set in snow. A leaden sky lowers over the troops of Herod breaking into houses, ignoring the pleas of desperate parents and dragging babies from distraught arms. Behind, more troops make escape impossible. While it can be argued that Bruegel set all his Biblical paintings in his own times and seasons, the events of the Duke of Alba's revenge on his fellow countrymen must have made their mark.

Bruegel's superb compositional handling of people is particularly noteworthy in *St John the Baptist preaching* (Budapest). In the background the small figure of the preacher is encircled by a compact crowd that broadens out to the colourfully dressed, well-formed shapes of the listeners at the back. Critics have seen in the face above the gypsy, partly obscured by the men with their backs to us, that of the painter himself.

Bruegel's sense of movement is so strong in *Wedding dance in the open air* (Detroit) that the rhythms of the dance have almost hidden the reason for it. In the far background, however, we can see the bride's crown pinned to a screen behind her place at table, while in the centre of the swirling movement, the groom holds the hand of the redhaired bride, the only woman not yet wearing the white bonnet of marriage.

The slower prelude to another wedding is depicted in *Wedding procession* (Brussels). Both wearing their wedding crowns, the bridegroom, seen between the tree trunks on the left, leads the column of men, while the bride, flanked by pages of honour, leads the women. The procession, whose solemnity is disturbed by the gossiping of the women and the anticipation of the meal by some of the men, makes its way towards the church, just visible through the trees, while behind stands the symbolic windmill and a suspicion of storms ahead in the dark cloud above.

The magnificent mountain landscape, arguably his most powerful, of an Alpine pass provides the road to Damascus for *The conversion of St Paul* (Vienna), a painting in which landscape and figures complement each other perfectly. Where the two axes of the painting meet — the line of the pass and the ridge along which the troops sent to persecute the Christians pass — lie a horse and its helpless rider, the blinded Saul who arose as Paul. The balance provided by the two horsemen results in a painting of great compositional power.

A totally different subject, *The land of Cockaigne* (Munich), demonstrates an equally complex and perfect composition. Here Bruegel returns to Netherlandish folklore to illustrate foolish man in the land of plenty. The images within the painting are of roundness, even the ground is round, and the shapes of the clerk, the superbly foreshortened soldier and the peasant, each represented by the symbols of his trade, form the spokes of a wheel that has been brought to a stop by gluttony and laziness.

Roundness is a feature of *The misanthrope* (Naples), but to rather different effect. Within the round shape, the inscription reads, 'As the world is treacherous I dress in mourning', and indeed the treacherous world of the round globe contains a thief stealing a purse from the misanthrope, who thinks that by isolating himself in his dark cloak against the world he cannot be hurt by it on his spiny way through life.

The parable of the blind (Naples) was inspired by Christ's parable, recorded both by St Matthew and St Luke, 'Can the blind lead the blind? Shall they not both fall into the ditch?' Within a beautiful landscape and portrayed in subtle and harmonious tones, the hard truth hits home. The six blind men, bound in misfortune, cannot ultimately help each other. The first has fallen, the others are bound to follow. The strong diagonal line moving from background to foreground reinforces the helplessness of these miserable men.

Equally dramatic is *The cripples* (Paris) whose composition has a monumentality that imbues the broad figures with an odd sense of dignity. Foxes' tails were symbolic of leprosy, which has suggested to some that these men were lepers, but others see a political parallel as the fox's brush was used as a symbol by anti-Spanish rebels for the Spanish governership of their country. Typically, Breugel gives rank to these unfortunates, their hats carrying the badges of the highest and lowest — a king, a bishop, a merchant, a soldier, and a peasant. No human being, he is saying, is immune from disease or vice.

Portraiture is rare in Breugel's work, so

two small works by him have their own mystery. Discovered in a castle on the banks of the Danube in the early 19th century, *Head of an old peasant woman* (Munich) may have been a study for *Dulle Griet*, while *Head of an old man* (Bordeaux) was for many years attributed to Bosch.

Magpie on the gallows (Darmstadt) is also a mystery, its meaning unclear. Karel van Mander, Breugel's first biographer, says that the painter left it to his wife with the statement that the magpie represents evil tongues, good for the gallows. Others have suggested that 'To dance under the gallows' is a variation of the saying, 'To dance on a volcano' and describes the political state of the Low Countries at this time. In a luminous landscape — one of Bruegel's most beautiful — where the light is given off by the trees in the foreground and builds to the plain beyond, diffusing finally in the far horizon, a peasant procession makes its dancing way towards the gallows, a reminder of the mortality of man.

Geographical Index of Paintings

Title Index of Paintings

THE PAINTINGS

The Netherlandish proverbs and detail (overleaf), 1559.
Oil on panel, 117 × 163 cm (46 × 64⅛ in).
Berlin, Kaiser Friedrich Museum.

IN EEN GHERIBBELT VLES, IN DANEN WATER
MET SLAPPEN EN GLIMPENDE, ICK BEN STAEN

INT SLAMPONDEN EN NEGEL MY NIEMANT VERKAN
AL OYST BI DE TIJSSEN, EN KE STELLEN IN DAS

T'HARNASCH SPOET MI EEN STOUTEN HAEN.
ICK HANGHE DE CRAY DE BELL AEN

NUS SOLDTEN WOERREN NEN HERES PYNT
ICK EN MACH NIET DIERN DAT DE SONNE INT WATER SCHY

Twelve Netherlandish proverbs (previous
page) and details (this page), 1558.
Oil on canvas, 74.5 × 98.4 cm
(29¼ × 38¾ in).
Antwerp, Museum Meyer Van den
Bergh.

View of Naples, c.1562-1563.
Oil on panel, 40 × 69.5 cm (15⅝ × 27⅜ in).
Rome, Doria Pamphili Gallery.

The battle between Carnival and Lent and detail (overleaf), 1559.

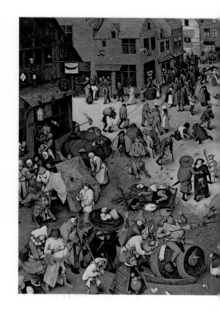

Oil on panel, 118 × 164.5 cm
(46½ × 64¾ in).
Vienna, Kunsthistorisches Museum.

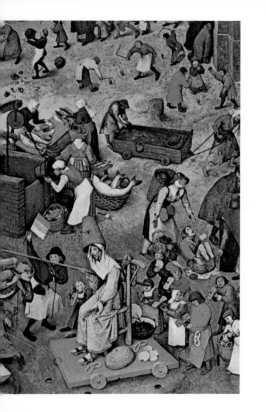

Children's games and detail (overleaf), 1560.
Oil on panel, 118 × 161 cm (46½ × 63⅜ in).
Vienna, Kunsthistorisches Museum.

Landscape with the fall of Icarus and detail (overleaf), *c.*1555-1558.

Oil on panel transferred to canvas,
73.5 × 112 cm (29 × 44½ in).
Brussels, Musées Royaux des Beaux Arts.

The battle between the Philistines and the Israelites
or *The judgement of Saul* 1562.
Oil on panel, 33.5 × 55 cm (13¼ × 21⅝ in).
Vienna, Kunsthistorisches Museum.

The fall of the rebel angels and details
(overleaf and pages 62-63), 1562.

Oil on panel, 117 × 162 cm
(46⅛ × 63¾ in).
Brussels, Musées Royaux des Beaux Arts.

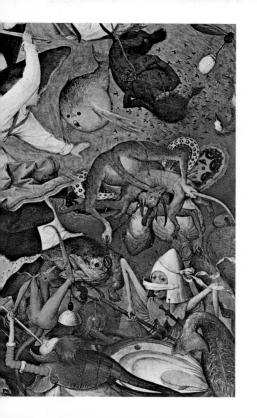

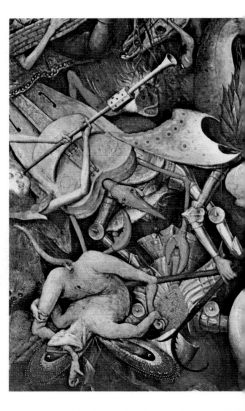

Two chained monkeys and detail (opposite), 1562.
Oil on panel, 20 × 23 cm (7⅞ × 9 in).
Berlin, Staatliche Museum.

The great tower of Babel 1563.
Oil on panel, 114 × 155 cm
(44$\frac{7}{8}$ × 61 in).
Vienna, Kunsthistorisches Museum.

The procession to Calvary and detail (overleaf), 1564.

Oil on panel, 124 × 170 cm
(48¾ × 66⅞ in).
Vienna, Kunsthistorisches Museum.

The Adoration of the Kings and details (below and overleaf), 1564.
Oil on panel, 111 × 83.5 cm (43¾ × 32¾ in).
London, National Gallery.

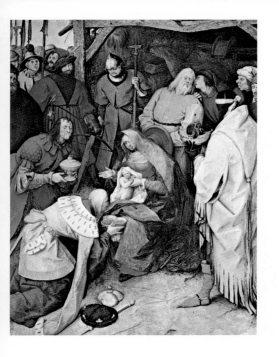

Hunters in the snow (December and January) and detail (overleaf), 1565.

Oil on panel, 117 × 162 cm
(46 × 63¾ in).
Vienna, Kunsthistorisches Museum.

Gloomy day (February and March) and detail (opposite and overleaf), 1565.
Oil on panel, 118 × 163 cm (46½ × 64⅛ in).
Vienna, Kunsthistorisches Museum.

Haymaking (June and July) and details
(overleaf and pages 88-89), 1565.

Oil on panel, 117 × 160 cm
(46 × 63⅜ in).
Prague, National Gallery.

Harvest (August and September) and
details (overleaf and pages 94-95), 1565.

x

90

Oil on panel, 118 × 160.5 cm
(46½ × 63¼ in).
New York, Metropolitan Museum.

The return of the herd (October and November) 1565.
Oil on panel, 117 × 156 cm
(46 × 62⅝ in).
Vienna, Kunsthistorisches Museum.

The triumph of death and details (overleaf and pages 102-103, 104, 105), c.1562.

Oil on panel, 117 × 162 cm
(46 × 63¾ in).
Madrid, Prado.

Dulle Griet ('Mad Meg') and details
(overleaf and pages 110-111),
c.1562-1563.

Oil on panel, 116 × 161 cm
(45¼ × 63⅜ in).
Antwerp, Museum Meyer Van den
Bergh.

The numbering at Bethlehem and detail
(overleaf), 1566.

Oil on panel, 116 × 164.5 cm
(45¼ × 64¾ in).
Brussels, Musées Royaux des Beaux Arts.

St John the Baptist preaching and detail (overleaf),
1566.
Oil on panel, 95 × 160.5 cm (37^3/$_8$ × 63^1/$_4$ in).
Budapest, Szepmuveszeti Museum.

116

Wedding dance in the open air 1566.
Oil on panel, 119 × 156 cm (47 × 62 in).
Detroit, Institute of Arts.

The massacre of the Innocents 1566.
Oil on panel, 111 × 160 cm
(43¾ × 63 in).
Vienna, Kunsthistorisches Museum.

Wedding procession and detail (overleaf), 1566.
Oil on panel, 61.5 × 114 cm (24¼ × 44⅞ in).
Brussels, Musée Communal du Roi.

The conversion of St Paul 1567.
Oil on panel, 108 × 156 cm.
(42½ × 61⅜ in).
Vienna, Kunsthistorisches Museum.

The land of Cockaigne or *The land of plenty* and details
(opposite and overleaf), 1567.
Oil on panel, 52 × 78 cm (20½ × 30¾ in).
Munich, Alte Pinakothek.

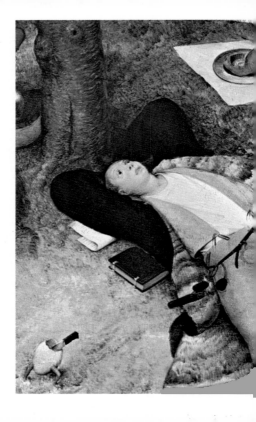

The misanthrope and detail (opposite), 1568.
Oil on canvas, 86 × 85 cm (33⁷/₈ × 33¹/₂ in).
Naples, National Museum (Capodimonte).

The parable of the blind and detail (overleaf), 1568.
Tempera on canvas, 86 × 154 cm
(33$\frac{7}{8}$ × 60$\frac{5}{8}$ in).
Naples, National Museum (Capodimonte).

Head of an old peasant woman and detail
(opposite), *c.*1568.
Oil on panel, 22 × 18 cm (8⅝ × 7¼ in).
Munich, Alte Pinakothek.

The magpie on the gallows and detail (opposite), 1568.
Oil on panel, 45.9 × 50.8 cm (18½ × 20 in).
Darmstadt, Hessisches Landesmuseum.

The peasant and the birdnester and detail (opposite),
1568.
Oil on panel, 59 × 68 cm (23¼ × 26¾ in).
Vienna, Kunsthistorisches Museum.

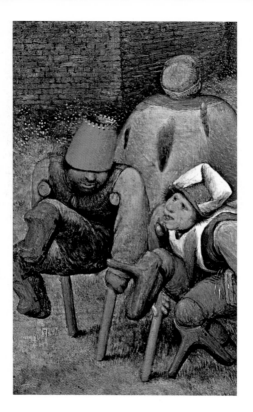

The cripples or *The lepers* and detail (opposite), 1568.
Oil on panel, 18 × 21.5 cm ($7\frac{1}{4}$ × $8\frac{1}{2}$ in).
Paris, Louvre.

Detail from *Peasant dance* (also overleaf), *c*.1567.
Oil on panel, 114 × 164 cm (44⅞ × 64⅝ in).
Vienna, Kunsthistorisches Museum.

Head of an old man and detail (opposite), 1568.
Oil on panel, diameter 18 cm (7¼ in).
Bordeaux, Musée des Beaux-Arts.

Peasant wedding and detail (overleaf),
c.1567.
Oil on panel, 114 × 163 cm
(44⅞ × 64⅝ in).
Vienna, Kunsthistorisches Museum.

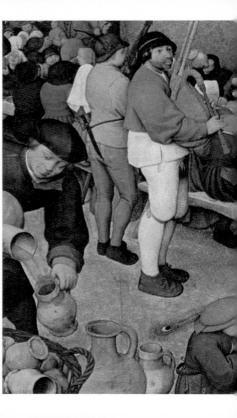

Storm at sea, c.1568.
Oil on panel, 70.5 × 97 cm
(27³/₄ × 38¹/₄ in).
Vienna, Kunsthistorisches Museum.